Virtual Incarnation?

And Other Sermons For Advent, Christmas, And Epiphany

William B. Kincaid, III

CSS Publishing Company, Inc., Lima, Ohio

VIRTUAL INCARNATION? AND OTHER SERMONS
FOR ADVENT, CHRISTMAS, AND EPIPHANY

Copyright © 2002 by
CSS Publishing Company, Inc.
Lima, Ohio

All rights reserved. No part of this publication may be reproduced in any manner whatsoever without the prior permission of the publisher, except in the case of brief quotations embodied in critical articles and reviews. Inquiries should be addressed to: Permissions, CSS Publishing Company, Inc., P.O. Box 4503, Lima, Ohio 45802-4503.

Scripture quotations are from the *New Revised Standard Version of the Bible*, copyright 1989 by the Division of Christian Education of the National Council of the Churches of Christ in the USA. Used by permission.

Library of Congress Cataloging-in-Publication Data

Kincaid, William B., 1960-
  Virtual incarnation? : and other sermons for Advent, Christmas, and Epiphany / William B. Kincaid III.
    p. cm.
Includes bibliographical references.
  ISBN 0-7880-1908-2 (pbk. : alk. paper)
  1. Advent sermons. 2. Christmas sermons. 3. Epiphany season—Sermons. 4. Christian Church (Disciples of Christ)—Sermons. 5. Sermons, American—20th century. I. Title.
  BV4254.5 .K56 2002
  252'.61—dc21   2002004123

For more information about CSS Publishing Company resources, visit our website at www.csspub.com or e-mail us at custserve@csspub.com or call (800) 241-4056.

ISBN 0-7880-1908-2   PRINTED IN U.S.A.

For my parents,
with love and thanksgiving

Table Of Contents

Preface   7

Sermons For Advent

1. Do We Want Christmas Back?   9
2. Things Look Different From Up Here   15
3. Gift-giving Of A Different Kind   21
4. Claiming Peace   27

Sermons For Christmas Eve

5. The Silent Word Is Pleading   33
6. Virtual Incarnation?   37

Sermons For Epiphany

7. Not A Word To Anyone   43
8. To Care And Not To Care   51
9. This Is My Life   57
10. I'll Take Two Of Whatever He Has   65

Preface

These sermons are offered with the hope that they will be experienced as a gift to the church. I appreciate the ongoing ministry of CSS Publishing and the work they do to make resources like this one available to those who offer leadership to the church.

Many of these sermons are based on lectionary texts. Others are topical sermons for the seasons of Advent, Christmas, and Epiphany that, I hope, are grounded in scripture and the tradition of the church.

Most of them were preached with the Woodland Christian Church (Disciples of Christ) in Lexington, Kentucky, where I have been privileged to serve as pastor since 1997. The stories which speak of congregational events and practices in this volume come from the life, worship, fellowship, and service of Woodland.

There are larger churches, churches with more elaborate buildings, and churches with more sophisticated programming, but I doubt that there are churches that are more welcoming and accepting than the one I presently serve. At Woodland, we understand diversity to be a means of knowing and experiencing God. We are put in touch with God's whole creation through our different experiences and perspectives. I am grateful for the journey we have made together thus far, for the care we have given each other, and for the anticipation of how the journey will unfold from here.

This collection of sermons came together during a time of great loss for me and my family. My mother passed away on the same day that I received the news that CSS would publish this book. I dedicate this book to her and to my father, with love and thanksgiving.

- 1 -

Do We Want Christmas Back?

How much do we really know about Jesus? Some information has been passed on to us through the biblical stories, but there are gaps in the information. For example, there's nothing in the stories we have in our Bible about when Jesus was born. Apparently it just wasn't much of an issue. Maybe some people knew, but they didn't bother to tell us. In those days, it was the date of the death of a person more than the date of birth that people remembered and commemorated.

Many think that there is a much better chance of Jesus' birth happening in the spring rather than in the winter, and the reason has to do with Luke's mention of shepherds "living in the fields, keeping watch over their flock by night" (Luke 2:8). Shepherds, we are told, only guarded their flocks day and night at lambing time, which was in the spring. In the winter time, the animals were kept in corrals, unwatched. This has led some to speculate that the actual time of Jesus' birth was the springtime.[1]

We don't know exactly when Jesus was born, but we do know how and when Christmas came to be celebrated on December 25. That story is a fascinating one. It was early in the fourth century. The excitement and crowds of religious people were at their peak, but it was not Christianity that was generating great excitement and drawing such great numbers of people. It was a pagan religion that was dominating life in the Roman Empire at that time, and it was so strong that it nearly threatened the existence and future of Christianity.

The Christian leaders of the day had an idea, one that was impressively clever. In fact, it was downright sneaky. The church folks looked around at the crowds of people celebrating the December 25 birthday of the sun god, Mithras, and decided to steal their holiday. The Christians decided to swipe the pagan's holiday right out from beneath them by having a Christian holiday at the same time the pagans were celebrating their holiday. So, over 300 years after Jesus was born, Christians began celebrating the birth of Jesus on December 25.[2]

Let's think again about what was going on there. December 25 was a pagan holiday. The Christians decided they would try to get in on a little of the action and decided to celebrate Jesus' birth on that day as well. Steal is too harsh a word, plus it would violate a commandment and we don't want to do that, but that is essentially how Christians got Christmas on December 25. We stole that day from the pagans! We took that holiday and redefined it and made it our own, and from that time on it was to be our day.

Somewhere along the way we let Christmas slip away. What happened is that some folks saw Christians celebrating the day of Jesus' birth, recognized an incredible opportunity for profit and gain and notoriety, and stole Christmas away from us. Commercialism actually may not have stolen Christmas away from us. We may have found the commercial aspects more appealing and understandable and simply decided to give Christmas away without a fight. It's time now to take Christmas back. And, if we have to steal it again to get it back, that's what we should do.

We are in a kind of a tug-of-war over Christmas right now and the winner will get to define what Christmas really means. On one end, pulling diligently on the Christmas rope, is a story that starts in scripture and has evolved through the tradition of the church. On the other end, an extravagant, excessive, retail-driven culture is pulling on the Christmas rope with the hope of defining it very differently from the Christian story. At least part of what Advent is for is to give us time to decide which side of the middle we are going to line up on. Advent is a time for us to think about what we want our Christmas celebration to look like, and feel like, and be about.

Let's think about how different these two sides of Christmas are. In the story that comes to us through scripture, we cannot escape the utter poverty of it all. Here are a couple of Jewish peasants away from home, surrounded by outcasts and smelly animals, preparing to have a baby in a stall somewhere. We romanticize that story to the point that we often miss the hardship of it all. It was more than rustic; it reeks of poverty.

But poverty seems strangely out of place in the way our culture tells the Christmas story. We know poverty still exists. We know the commercials and advertisements must make those in need feel even worse about their situation, but Christmas from the retailer's point of view is about selling things to us, even if we don't need them. It's about believing that the dollar has the power to fill an aching void or mend a strained relationship or raise the self-esteem of ourselves and others.

Not many of us are hoping to become really poor just in time for Christmas. That's not the point. The point is that these are two very different ways to experience Christmas. Scripture warns us not to place our faith in things, but also warns us against how things can distort our faith. "Blessed are the poor," Jesus says (Luke 6:20), but not because being poor is so great. It's not. The poor are blessed in that their faith remains in God and is unencumbered and unaffected by the trappings that ensnare the rest of us at times.

In the story that comes to us through scripture, we cannot escape the sense of upheaval. When Jesus' mother was pregnant with him, she talked about upheaval. "God has scattered the proud in the thoughts of their hearts. God has brought down the powerful from their thrones. God has lifted up the lowly, filled the hungry with good things, and sent the rich away empty" (Luke 1:51-53). The Gospel lesson for the first Sunday of Advent each year talks about the shaking of heaven and earth and people being caught in fear and foreboding. Later, upheaval becomes central in Jesus' ministry. What finally led to his death was that he wouldn't leave things alone, but instead constantly called attention to abuses of power and neglect of the needy and self-righteousness on the part of the religious folks of the day.

Upheaval, however, isn't a part of the Christmas vocabulary of our culture. It's a time for gathering around the fire, smoothing things over, even glossing over the pain of some situations. If we trusted the commercials, we would think that all the problems of our city and world have been solved. There's no sign of conflict or exclusion or oppression. That kind of advertising can lull us into complacency and indifference. When we are persuaded to believe that everybody is doing okay, the whole Christmas message of Jesus coming to offer hope and healing and wholeness to the world doesn't seem to matter that much anymore.

Most of us probably don't wake up every morning asking ourselves how much trouble we can cause today, but there is something about the gospel news that is troubling. Something about the gospel invites us to create upheaval in those situations where people are being treated unfairly and children are going hungry and hatred and prejudice are spreading. We may sing "O little town of Bethlehem, how still we see thee lie," but the news from Bethlehem is that change is on the way. Do we want Christmas back if it is going to mean that kind of disruption to our lives and to our world?

It's a tug-of-war between the manger and the mall and the winner gets to say what Christmas will be like. On one side, people of faith are saying that this is a time to prepare and to savor. It's a time of patient waiting and anticipation. On the other side, our throwaway culture preaches the promises of immediate gratification.

One year a congregation decided to prepare its own Advent devotional booklet rather than buying copies of one from a religious supplier. The booklet included a devotion for each day of the Advent season; all the thoughts were written by members of that church. However, the people did not practice the Advent discipline of waiting. Many people reported that they read through the entire booklet as soon as they got it, which was a week before Advent even started.

The people also reported that they were very moved by what they read. Some spoke of Christmas and life without their parents. Some spoke of Christmas as a time to take in a needy child from school. Some spoke of what Christmas was like during their tours of duty in World War II. Some spoke of the many changes, wanted and unwanted, that have occurred through the years.

Many of the devotions described less-than-perfect circumstances, yet they still proclaimed hope and joy and peace and love. Every devotion called the people back to those things which Advent promises to us. Each day's reflection led the members and friends of that congregation to take whatever preparation time was necessary in order to make those things a part of their lives.

In both the words and in between the lines it was evident that those people wanted Christmas back, and most of us are no different. The trappings are fine and we will enjoy them. The gifts are nice and they will be symbols of our love and appreciation for each other. But at some deep level, we want Christmas back.

We don't want it to be defined just by our purchasing power, or just by the tendencies of a consumer culture, or just by the needs of retail stores to move their merchandise. We want the experience of Christmas to be richer, deeper, more lasting. We want to celebrate an ancient birth and at the same time receive the newness of the promise of that birth. As the days grow shorter in the northern hemisphere, we are longing for the light of the world to shine upon us and in us and through us. We want Christmas back.

And so we are invited into this season of preparation to sort out our lives, to identify our real hope, to claim its real meaning. We are invited to take time daily to watch and wait, to cultivate an active hope, to think and reflect, to talk with the people around us, so that at least as far as we are concerned Christmas takes on a distinctively Christian witness to God's love for us all.

Two divorcing parents came before a judge for the custody hearing concerning their son. The man was Christian and the woman was Jewish. She had asked that their son be with her for the Jewish holy days. Thinking that was fair enough, the man made a similar request. He asked that his son be with him for Christmas and Easter. That request was denied because, as the judge said, "Christmas and Easter are not Christian holidays anymore." One judge doesn't make it so, but there are signs elsewhere that Christmas belongs to someone else these days.

Advent is a time for our waiting, but we aren't the only ones waiting. There is One who is waiting for us. Waiting to see what we will do with this complex season. Waiting to see if we will prepare ourselves. Waiting to see if we really want Christmas back.

---

1. Charles Panati, *Sacred Origins of Profound Things: The Stories Behind the Rites and Rituals of the World's Religions* (New York: Penguin Books, 1996), p. 215.

2. See Panati, pp. 215-217.

- 2 -

Things Look Different From Up Here

Isaiah 2:1-5

Things look different from up here.

In the movie *Dead Poets Society*, Professor Keating, who was played by Robin Williams, teaches English in an all-male prep school. In fact, it is the prep school which the good professor had attended years earlier. As a young man, the professor had left a legacy as a nonconformist, one who marched to the beat of a different drum. However, the professor had gone on to be a Rhodes Scholar and was exceptionally qualified to teach in this prestigious school.

Professor Keating's colleagues were all much older, much more experienced, and rather set in their ways. The role of tradition weighed heavily. Things had worked well for 150 years; why do anything differently now? It is not unusual for change to be received with some hesitance and resistance, even when it may be for the better. However, in a school where tradition was the guiding force, anything that did not conform to the standards in place was looked upon with grave suspicion.

It was into this atmosphere that Professor Keating's rather unorthodox teaching methods were introduced. One day, while listening to a symphony, the students and the professor wore blindfolds. Perhaps that allowed them to hear in a way that was otherwise not possible. Another day, the professor took his students outside and had three of them walk around in a circle while the rest of the students watched. Just as the professor thought, even though the three had distinctly different walks at the beginning of the exercise, by the time he told them to stop they all had amazingly similar walks. From this, he warned the students against a dull conformity which saps creativity, and then encouraged them to walk around in their own styles of walking. For a moment they walked as unique individuals that had been set free from other people's expectations.

By far the most compelling day of class was when Professor Keating stood on top of his desk, and not only Professor Keating, but the whole class, one by one, came to stand on top of that desk. You can imagine that a few were scratching their heads in bewilderment, wondering why in the world the professor was wasting valuable class time by having students come and stand on top of his desk. The answer was simple. In the words of Professor Keating, "Things look different from up here."

We won't ask for a show of hands, but we have to ask: Has anybody stood on top of a desk lately and looked around? When was the last time we saw things from a different perspective? When was the last time that we stood where others stand and saw things as they see them? When was the last time we shed the very natural blinders that develop and viewed the world from a new position?

Joe and Beth commuted into the city every day for work. Several different routes would take them from their home on the north side of the city to their work locations on the south side. While it was not the quickest or easiest route, they often would choose a combination of streets that led them through some of the poorest, most crime-ridden neighborhoods in their town.

Joe and Beth had been very fortunate in their lives. Both had grown up in a very safe small town and had lived rather sheltered lives even after moving to the city. Their professional lives had provided a standard of living well beyond anything they had been able to imagine. The year they built their sprawling new house on the northern edge of the city, they had a life-deepening experience. That summer they had volunteered their time and energy to help build a Habitat for Humanity house in a neighborhood that had a reputation for drugs and violence.

When Joe and Beth took possession of their new home, it became all the more urgent and important for them to travel through that troubled neighborhood once or twice a week, either on their way to work or on their way home. It would have been comfortable for them to kick back and relax in a house whose walls didn't have the first fingerprint on them yet. It would have been easy for them to assume that everybody else must live this way. So every once in a while Joe and Beth would drive through that poor, crime-ridden neighborhood where they had seen firsthand the struggles that some people face. It was Joe's and Beth's way of standing on top of the desk and looking around. And when they did, the professor's words rang true: Things really do look different.

Isaiah wanted people to get out of their comfortable chairs and view things from the desktop. In fact, that wasn't even enough for Isaiah. What Isaiah really wanted was for people to travel up the mountain of God and see things as God sees them. Isaiah talked a lot about the coming of the Messiah, saying that when the Messiah comes a new age will be inaugurated and things will look different. Isaiah was convinced that the coming of the Messiah will cause swords and spears and weapons to be used in the raising of crops and in providing people with food, rather than for dividing one nation against another. And what will be taught and learned on the mountain of God will not be war and division, but the ways of God — peace and harmony and cooperation (Isaiah 2:4).

In another place, Isaiah says that when the Messiah comes the oppression of people will end, the oppressor's rod will be broken, and people will live with a sense of justice — not vengeance, not greed, but justice (Isaiah 9:2-7). Isaiah also said that when the Messiah comes the meek and poor of the earth will get their fair portion and endless fighting between people will cease in a way so surprising that it might be compared to a wolf living with a lamb, or a lion and a calf cohabitating (Isaiah 11:1-9).

In still another place, Isaiah says that when the Messiah comes the downtrodden of this world will be exalted and the proud, self-righteous folks will be humbled, almost like valleys being lifted up and mountains being made low. For when the Messiah comes, all of the people will stand on equal, level ground and together be showered with the glory of the Lord (Isaiah 40:1-5).

Isaiah says, "Stand up on that desk. God is calling you to take a fresh perspective, to look at things in a new way." And what a great way to begin that passage: "In the days to come." Isaiah knew things weren't right yet, but he was able to envision the time when things would be right. Isaiah's "In the days to come" is a cousin to Dr. King's "I have dream." Both phrases invite us to envision that coming day when peace and justice will prevail.

Even if God were to be worshiped everywhere, there was something special about the mountain. For Isaiah the mountain was an image that called people back to the giving of the law and reminded people that God sees things differently than we do and wants things to be different than they are. Advent is the time when we yearn for things to be the way God wants them to be. Advent is an invitation to go up to the mountain of God.

"Things look different from up here." That is God's promise for all who are troubled, confused, uncertain, hurting, and for all who are dragging behind them heavy burdens of various kinds. God says, "Up here you can see better the peace I have for you, the direction I have promised to you, the healing I am sending. Up here it is more readily evident that frustration and brokenness do not have the final word. Up here it is more obviously apparent that profound hope is close at hand. Up here it is easy to see that release is ahead from the burdens in your life." Come, let us go up to the mountain of God. Things look different up here. That's a promise for those of us who need a promise like that to get us through.

But it is also a challenge. Things look different up here, and that calls us to a certain kind of living. On the mountain of God, peace takes priority over war, the interests of the community shape our lives more than our self-interests, and the hope of a new day and a new way springs eternal. On the mountain of God, there are no walls separating people and no ceilings holding people down. Prejudice and hate are not taught or accepted there.

We are called and sent to make the rest of the world look like the mountain of God, a world where little children are not abused, where the elderly are not forgotten, and where discrimination of every form comes to an end; a world where those who have never been given much of a chance receive a fresh start; a world where the lonely find comfort, the weary find strength, and the left-out experience affirmation.

God calls us to find and visit the mountain in our lives, to spend time in that place where we are given the gift of seeing things differently. We can experience that in many ways. We might begin by having a conversation with a child. It doesn't really matter about what, but talk with a child about something. It's a mountaintop experience because it invariably provides the blessing of a different perspective.

Or we might share a meal with some people who are homeless. It can be a turkey dinner with all its fixings during the holidays, or just a pimento cheese sandwich on the curb of a street on most any day. It's a mountaintop experience. Everything changes. Or we could visit a nursing home, or open the pages of scripture, or actually go to a place, whether it is hilly or not, where things can be sorted out and seen for what they really are, and where God can be known and experienced for who God really is.

For the world that God envisions is different. It is a better world than the world we often experience. The world God is weaving into existence even now is a world of peace and hope, love and joy. Some days it is hard to see that side of things with the angle we have, so God gives us a fresh angle. We are positioned for a new perspective where we can see things differently, as they really are. Not even standing on a desk adequately serves the purpose once we have been to the mountain of God.

- 3 -

Gift-giving Of A Different Kind

It is one congregation's practice to celebrate the twelve days of the Christmas season by making a difference in at least one child's life during each of those twelve days. During Advent the members and friends of the congregation bring gifts to the church to support announced causes, everything from children in foster care to teens in juvenile detention centers. An area in the fellowship hall marked "Twelve Days of Christmas" is reserved so that people can place their gifts there. Volunteers distribute those gifts to social service agencies, hospitals, group homes, and community resource centers.

One year on the Sunday night before Christmas the congregation had gathered for a fellowship dinner. As might be expected, a large man in a red suit made an appearance in the fellowship hall and brought gifts for the children of the church. Saint Nicholas gathered the children around him and told stories. He later took each child on his lap and listened intently as the boys and girls expressed their wishes. Before climbing down from Saint Nicholas' lap, all the boys and girls received a nicely-wrapped gift. It was a book of stories from the Christmas season.

The dinner concluded that night. People began to collect their dishes and say their good-byes when something near the gift area caught their eye. One by one the children who had received gifts from the church, by way of Saint Nicholas, were placing their books of Christmas stories with the gifts for the Twelve Days of Christmas. All who witnessed that had their own spirit of giving transformed.

We all have experienced the exhilaration of giving a thoughtfully-selected gift to someone. The expression on the other person's face conveys appreciation and thanksgiving. We also know the frustration of gift-giving. We've seen those other expressions as well, reactions which essentially say either "What is it?" or "What possessed you to buy that for me?"

Gift-giving can be exasperating. It can also be very expensive, especially in those years when the demand of the season's hottest doll or toy or game drives the price up while people scurry from mall to mall as if on a mission from God in search of that must-have item. Then there's the challenge of buying for people who at least appear to have everything already. Sometimes we can't imagine what it is that other people don't already have.

Gift certificates are always a possibility. We may not know exactly what to give some people, so we give gift certificates that both show our fondness for them and allow them to eat at restaurants and shop at stores they might not otherwise frequent. Those are nice gifts.

Then there's the matter of money, giving cold, hard cash. Few of us turn down the gift of U.S. currency. Sometimes cash can get us out of a tight spot in a hurry, but most importantly it gives people the freedom to get what they want and need. It is especially nice when we aren't up to date on exactly what would make the perfect gift for a great-great-niece, twice removed, who lives five states away.

Gift-giving isn't an easy thing. Sometimes it is not only finding the right gift in the right color and size that complicates matters, but also the expectations involved. "Will she like this?" "Is he expecting something different or something more?" "Will they think less of me if I give this?" "Will this be enough to make our children happy?" So many unnecessary emotions cloud the picture; at least they are unnecessary if we already share a good, loving relationship with the people receiving our gifts. With those people, we know that their presence will always mean more than any presents we might give or receive.

The group known as Alternatives in Ellenwood, Georgia, provides ideas about alternative gift-giving. The hope is to offer ideas that ease some of the stress and worry of the season. One year, all of the articles from the Alternatives gift-giving guide were based on the words of Jesus: "My peace I give to you. I do not give to you as the world gives. Do not let your hearts be troubled."

Those words of Jesus call us to a different kind of giving. Much of our world gives in a very packaged, impersonal way. Some people find great comfort in being able to walk into any Wal-Mart or McDonald's or some other chain anywhere in the country to find exactly the same store, regardless of the location, but we lose something when every part of the country begins to look like every other part of the country. We lose a sense of local flavor and particularity. We lose a feel for how rich the diversity is from region to region. But this is the way most of the world gives, which means that we have to be on guard that our own giving doesn't take on that kind of bland flatness.

A different kind of gift-giving would cause us to step back and think. For example, what would change if we asked of each person on our gift list, "Who is this person to me?" That's a powerful question. We can ask the easier question, "Who is this person?" and never really get at the heart of gift-giving joy. Consider how different those questions are and how they change our attitude and spirit and gift selection during the Christmas season.

"Who is this person to me?" connects us with the most enduring and endearing parts of our relationship with one another. Think how that question can change completely how we approach what is sometimes a burdensome task. More than just mother or father or brother or sister or friend, more than just daughter or son or grandchild or grandparent, the question "Who is this person to me?" invites us to reflect on what the person means to us and how our relationship with the person brings out the best in us.

Rather than just picking out a necktie for Dad and then quickly moving to the next department for another selection, consider who Dad is to you. If he has been the one who has instilled a keen sense of right and wrong and who adamantly instructed you to respect other people, that should offer some ideas for a gift that expresses appreciation for those things. If your daughter is someone from whom you have learned about second chances and tireless hopefulness, that should offer some clues as well. Think about the people in your life. Who are those people to you?

And once we have answered that question, maybe we can imagine gifts that will be symbols of our love and appreciation for them. Maybe we want to make at least one of our gifts something that expresses what these people mean to us. Plenty of very useful, practical gifts still will be exchanged this year, but perhaps among them can be things that reveal to our loved ones who they are to us. It's giving of a different kind.

Another layer to this alternative giving comes in a much less tangible and much less material form. Maybe we need to give someone the gift of a second chance. Maybe we need to give our church the gift of a positive attitude. Maybe we need to give the people around us the gift of laughter and an easy spirit. Maybe we need to give our community something of our time. Maybe we need to give somebody our forgiveness. Sometimes our gift-giving needs to include giving to some people things we really may not want to give, things like patience, kindness, understanding, and cooperation. Gift-giving of a different kind.

Sometimes we need to be generous with ourselves. Maybe we need to give ourselves a new dose of strength and peace during hard days. Maybe we need to give ourselves permission to have a good time. Maybe we need to give ourselves the gift of knowing we have done our best. Giving of a different kind.

And let's remember how our giving can impact so many lives. For people who seem to have everything, a wonderful way to honor who they are to us is to give to their alma mater or to a community agency in their name. Eight dollars provides food and emergency shelter for a day at a homeless center. Twenty-five dollars will buy some new chairs for the dining hall at a church camp. Fifty dollars to Habitat for Humanity will put a door on a new house for a deserving family. Giving of a different kind.

The One we worship is the most radical of alternative givers. Somewhere in the mind of God the question surfaced, "Who are these people to me?" And finally God answered, "My very own, these people are my very own. I'll give them a part of myself."

A story titled "The Small White Envelope" is one wife's story about how their practice of gift-giving transformed their family life and their celebration of Christmas.[1]

"It's just a small, white envelope stuck among the branches of our Christmas tree. No name, no identification, no inscription. It has peeked through the branches of our tree for the past ten years or so. It all began because my husband Mike hated Christmas. Oh, not the true meaning of Christmas, but the commercial aspects of it — the overspending, the frantic running around at the last minute to get a tie for Uncle Harry and the dusting powder for Grandma — you know, the gifts given in desperation because you couldn't think of anything else.

"Knowing he felt this way, I decided one year to bypass the usual shirts, sweaters, ties, and so forth. I reached for something special just for Mike. The inspiration came in an unusual way. Our son Kevin, who was twelve years old that year, was wrestling at the junior level at the school he attended. Shortly before Christmas, there was a non-league match against a team sponsored by an inner-city church. These youngsters were dressed in sneakers so ragged that shoestrings seemed to be the only thing holding them together. Their attire presented a sharp contrast to our boys in their spiffy blue and gold uniforms and sparkling new wrestling shoes.

"As the match began, I was alarmed to see that the other team was wrestling without headgear. It was a luxury the opposing team obviously could not afford. Well, we ended up walloping them. We took every weight class. Mike, seated beside me, shook his head sadly, 'I wish just one of them could have won,' he said. 'They have a lot of potential, but losing like this could take the heart right out of them.'

"Mike loved kids — all kids — and he understood them, having coached little league football, baseball, and lacrosse. That's when the idea for his present came. That afternoon, I went to a local sporting goods store and bought an assortment of wrestling headgear and shoes and sent them anonymously to the inner-city church. On Christmas Eve, I placed an envelope on the tree with a note inside telling Mike what I had done and that this was his gift from me.

"His smile was the brightest thing about Christmas that year and in succeeding years. For each Christmas, I followed the tradition — one year sending a group of mentally handicapped youngsters to a hockey game; another year a check to a pair of elderly brothers whose home had burned to the ground the week before Christmas, and on and on.

"The envelope became the highlight of our Christmas. It was always the last thing opened on Christmas morning and our children, ignoring their new toys, would stand with wide-eyed anticipation as their dad lifted the envelope from the tree to reveal its contents. As the children grew, the toys gave way to more practical presents, but the envelope never lost its allure.

"Last year we lost Mike to a dreaded cancer. When Christmas rolled around, I was still so wrapped in grief that I barely got the tree up. But Christmas Eve found me placing an envelope on the tree before I went to bed. When I awoke the next morning, there were three more envelopes on the tree. Each of our children, unbeknownst to the others, had placed an envelope on the tree for their dad. The tradition has grown and someday will expand even further with our grandchildren standing to take down the envelope."

Gift-giving of a different kind.

---

1. The source of this story is uncertain. It was passed on to me by a member of the congregation I serve.

- 4 -

Claiming Peace

Don't we wonder sometimes why there isn't more peace than there is? Few themes in scripture are mentioned more often than peace. If asked, almost everybody would say that peace is a good thing. We pour lots of resources into peacemaking, everything from a bumper sticker that says, "Make peace, not war," to staffing government and private offices around the world with ambassadors and mediators and negotiators.

But when we look around, peace has escaped us. It is estimated by the Carter Center in Atlanta that at any given time fifty wars are going on in the world. Many of these are tribal conflicts in remote areas, but I'm sure if one broke out in our region of the world we wouldn't think of it as minor. Violence sweeps through what ought to be peaceful homes, and during the holidays domestic abuse soars. Enough assaults happen in schools and church parking lots and shopping malls and neighborhoods to remind us that peace is very elusive.

So if we agree that peace is a good thing, why isn't there more of it? One reason is because so many people are angry these days. We recognize in the phenomenon of road rage how much anger people are living with. With this anger so close to the surface, people fly off the handle over practically nothing.

Anger can be used in such a positive, constructive way to make a better world. Scripture encourages us to be angry, but to not sin (Ephesians 4:26). Many situations call for a righteous anger that will address the problems of suffering children and manipulated seniors and unfair situations all around our community, but most of what we are seeing is nothing like that. Instead, it is anger that is waiting to pick a fight, stir up a controversy, embarrass a community leader, or blame someone else for one's own problems. It seems to grow out of a deep-seated personal misery, and it is very vengeful. Peace has a difficult time flourishing when that kind of anger is in play.

Another reason that peace eludes us, especially in this country, is that we are not very good at talking about really difficult issues. Instead of bringing some understanding, tolerance, and humility to a table of discussion, we allow volatile issues to divide and polarize us. One person noted on a Kentucky Education Television program that the Kentucky State Legislature cannot get anything significant done because they are stuck on the four G's: God, guns, gays, and gynecology. That pretty well sums it up in many states around the country. A lot of needed legislation is buried beneath proposals about school prayer (God), the availability and need for weapons (guns), the private lives of gays, and abortion-related issues (gynecology).

It's hard to have peace when we make our love of neighbor contingent on whether he agrees with us on capital punishment or on whether she agrees with us on school vouchers. Sometimes we are unnecessarily threatened by disagreement. Instead of listening to each other for ways that our pieces of the truth can be complemented by the pieces of truth that someone else may bring, we lash out at those who disagree with us and demonize those who hold positions different from our own. What often happens in the absence of honest debate and spirited dialogue is that we begin to attack each other. Jesus didn't expect us to agree with each other on everything. He did expect us to find ways to love each other, regardless of where we stand on divisive issues.

Perhaps the most bizarre thing is when we are forced to change our positions on something because we find that our enemy agrees with us. The classic example is when Hillary Rodham Clinton published a book and gave all the proceeds to charity. The book was based on that wonderful African proverb which reminds us that we all play a role in raising and nurturing children. Where would any of us be without the love and guidance of parents, ministers, youth leaders, choir directors, Sunday school teachers, school teachers and administrators, scout troops, close friends, concerned citizens, volunteers, nurses, firefighters, social workers, police officers, and hundreds of other people?

Yet, for some reason, when Ms. Clinton published her book, *It Takes A Village*, all kinds of people attacked the idea as if it were a new wave of communism. Peace cannot happen if we are more committed to maintaining an adversarial relationship than we are to being open to glimpses of the truth. It's a hard thing to swallow sometimes, but we will learn far more from people who disagree with us than from those who already agree with us. If we are so entrenched as enemies that we cannot see that, the possibility of peace diminishes greatly.

Another reason that peace is hard to come by is that we learn early on to hold on to what is ours. It is a hard lesson to unlearn. Sometimes the turf-protecting is political. In the Middle East, violence erupts every so often because millions of people with very different views are trying to live on the same little piece of ground. Racial equality is slowed down terribly because it would threaten the influence some of us have by granting whites and blacks and browns and yellows and reds an equal voice.

Often the turf-protecting comes in the form of wanting to take credit for an accomplishment. Few things get in the way of good things happening like people needing to be acknowledged for their work. The movie *And the Band Played On* gives strong evidence that part of the delay in diagnosing the cause of AIDS was due to two researchers who both wanted credit for the discovery. A lot of people were infected and died because two doctors did not share their work with one another.

We see the same kinds of things happen in government, where partisanship stalls the work of the people in government. It happens in churches as well, where the need for being recognized stands in the way of things moving ahead. We all do more than we get credit for. Besides, if we are in it for the credit we won't last long. The most important ministry we will do in this life will be things that most people will never know about.

A lot of talk about peace, but not enough peace to go along with the talk. So what can we do? First, we commit ourselves today to claiming peace, regardless of what is going on around us. Perfect circumstances are rare in this world, so in the midst of the challenges and messiness and changes and conflicts, we are left to claim whatever peace we can.

The story is told of a wealthy benefactor who once commissioned two artists to paint a portrait of peace. One painted what we might expect: a pastoral scene of a calm mountain lake, flanked by rolling hills against a background of majestic mountains. The other painted a similar setting, but under quite different conditions. It featured an ominous sky filled with angry clouds, trees bent beneath the force of a mighty wind, and the lake choppy with turbulent waves. In the foreground, the careful eye could see a small bird going on with its life in the midst of the harshness and violence.[1]

We are that small bird, called to a life of peace in the midst of the brokenness and incompleteness. And we are called to the richest form of peace. The Hebrew word for peace, *shalom*, means so much more than the absence of conflict. It means wholeness. Shalom is that experience wherein we are blessedly content and assured, even when the circumstances say we have no reason to be.

Several years ago someone passed along this warning: Be on the lookout for symptoms of inner peace. Here are some of the signs. 1) An unmistakable ability to enjoy each moment. 2) A loss of interest in judging other people. 3) A loss of the ability to worry. This is a very serious symptom of inner peace. 4) Frequent attacks of smiling. 5) An increased susceptibility to the love of others and the urge to return that love.

This is a peace that grows from the inside out. Contrary to the message of our culture that tells us peace will come on the inside when we have the right things on the outside of our lives, God's gift of peace begins within and grows outwardly. And the longer we are still, and the more often we listen for it, and the more willing we are to receive, that peace will grow within us.

The second thing we do is to make sure that this inside-out peace makes it to the outside. Our peace is not something we sit on, but something we implement in the world, on earth as it is in heaven, if you will. Jesus said that the peacemakers are blessed (Matthew 5:9), and then he must have turned to his disciples and said, "You are one, and you are one, and you are one. You are all peacemakers if you are following me."

In the Greek, the word for peacemakers actually means founders of peace. Think of all the places that are in need of finding some peace. That is the work to which we are called, to allow our inside-out peace to create so much hope within us that we dare to move into the conflicted, oppressed parts of our relationships, our homes, our church, our community, and establish peace. We claim peace for ourselves in the midst of less-than-perfect circumstances, and then we claim peace in our world in places where people aren't able to envision or experience it yet.

On November 4, 1995, Israeli Prime Minister Yitzhak Rabin was gunned down by a law student. The assassination happened, of all times, at the conclusion of a peace rally in Tel Aviv. An estimated one hundred thousand people had celebrated peace that day with the Prime Minister. After singing the "Song of Peace," Rabin had placed the paper with the lyrics in his coat pocket. Within minutes, an assassin's bullet penetrated that pocket, leaving the words to the "Song of Peace" drenched in blood.

Mr. Rabin had been a tough soldier and a powerful founder of peace. He had survived three wars and had attained the rank of General. In 1994, he shared the Nobel Peace Prize with Yasir Arafat. Both Israel and the rest of the world were reminded not only of the depth of grief, but also of how unwelcome and unpopular peacemakers are. They seem to be targets for malcontents.

Abe Pollin was one of the many Americans who attended Mr. Rabin's funeral. At the time, there was a National Basketball Association team named the Washington Bullets. Mr. Pollin owned that team. Some probably used that name "Bullets" without giving it much thought, but when Mr. Pollin returned from Israel he announced, "My friend Yitzhak Rabin was shot in the back by bullets. The name Bullets is no longer appropriate for a sports team. The Bible says that if you save one life, you save the world.

Hopefully, we will save many more than that." Now Mr. Pollin's team is named the Washington Wizards.[2]

We are called to be peacemakers, and everything from the name of our favorite sports team to the toys and video games we play with to our involvement on issues of peace and safety in our community can be measurements of where we are on that journey. In all things, for the sake of our lives and God's world, let us claim peace. And let us not only make it our own, but let us be such devoted witnesses to peace that others see it as a compelling alternative and an attractive solution to the challenges before us.

---

1. Larry Paul Jones, *Biblical Preaching Journal*, Spring 1995, p. 21.

2. G. Curtis Jones and Paul H. Jones, *500 Illustrations: Stories from Life for Preaching and Teaching* (Nashville: Abingdon Press, 1998), pp. 174-175.

- 5 -

The Silent Word Is Pleading

The silent Word is pleading. That's a line from the hymn "What Child Is This," but how many of us have given that phrase much thought? Tonight we are reminded of the power of silence, and the force of truth, and the persuasion of purity. And tonight, we engage in a more concerted, more focused effort to make room for the One whose mere presence, without yet speaking a word, brings light and life to the world and all who dwell therein. For the One who comes tonight cuts through the clutter of words thrown around in excess and carelessness, and drowns out our world's loud noises with his silence. The silent Word is pleading.

Sometimes words aren't needed, and sometimes words detract instead of enhance. Sometimes they get in the way, attempting to describe mysteries that are beyond words. And in this time of lost civility, we have forgotten how powerful words are. Cruel, harsh words are hurled over airwaves by talk show hosts at the public figures they despise the most. Words like that diminish all of us by fostering a climate of suspicion and divisiveness.

People who participate regularly in silent retreats say that they experience God in new ways as a result of that time spent in silence. They also tell us that they see themselves and their world in new ways as well. What is there in our lives that we would appreciate more if we were silent for a day? Would it be the blue skies, or the squirrels who play in the yard, or the hundreds of conveniences we enjoy, or the people with whom we laugh and cry and play and pray?

Our expressions and gestures often say more than our words. To preach in the African-American tradition is to receive constant verbal feedback, but every tradition includes rich and poignant feedback during the preaching event. Almost every minister has received all kinds of messages while preaching. They include nods of agreement that shout, "Go, Sister," as well as perplexed looks that ask, "What you talking about, Brother?" Occasionally there is a facial warning that says, "Don't go there, Preacher." Just because no words have been spoken doesn't mean nothing has been communicated.

And tonight, when the silent Word is pleading, we think of other times when in silence the message is communicated in ways more clearly than words ever could. We have seen the reprimanding frown of a mother and without anything being verbalized we got the message. We have looked into the eye of a lover and felt his smile fall upon us and without a word, affection was spoken. We have arrived at the emergency room only to be met with expressions of horror and shock and knew immediately that the news was not good.

We have walked down nursing home corridors lined with loneliness and have heard the cries of residents before they ever opened their mouths. We have watched homeless people in city parks shuffling their way to nowhere and have heard sounds of hopelessness echoing off every tree.

But for every silent source of despair, for every problem that goes unnamed, for every concern that is either unspoken or is too heavy for words to describe, a baby is born in Bethlehem. The Word became flesh. And long before that Word ever told a parable or prayed a prayer or welcomed a sinner or held a child or healed a paralytic, that Word rested in silence in a manger.

Of all the loud and obvious ways to make a point, ways which as often as not turn us off, ours is a subtle God who comes in the understatement of a child and in the stillness of a starry night. The silent Word is pleading. Hope emanates from that silence, and peace, and joy, and love. Loud-clashing cymbals are saved for another day, as are burning bushes and rolling thunder and mighty winds.

For the loudest noise on this night is simply the silence of it all, and the one who makes the grandest announcement is the One who is yet to speak.

One so pure, one whose light shines so brightly, one whose love is all embracing, one whose truth is so compelling, has little need for words. This One is the Word.

And for all who are hurting and lonely and afraid, for all who are trapped in poverty by unjust systems, for all who long to be loved and made whole, for all who dare to dream of a more fulfilling, more abundant way, and yes, for people like you and me and for a world like ours, the silent Word is pleading.

- 6 -

Virtual Incarnation?

Word has it that giving birth is a messy thing. We have been with folks just prior to a baby being delivered and have seen the emotional messiness. So many thoughts must be running through a mother-to-be's mind — excitement about bringing a new life into the world, fear of anything that might go wrong, and maybe most of all relief at finally having a baby that she has carried for nine months.

And there's the physical messiness, the kind of thing that causes many of us to turn our heads when a birth is shown on television's "The Learning Channel." There's some water and blood, and some stretching and tearing. Babies look so sweet and innocent soon after they are born, but at birth there's some cleaning up to do.

Whatever else we want to make of tonight, however we want to celebrate, regardless of how much we romanticize the manger scene with the animals, the storyline tonight is of a baby being born and all the messiness that goes with that. Think about a pregnant Mary anticipating the day of delivery, experiencing her labor contractions, finding a place where she could lie down. It was her first child, and as a rule the labor is longer and the birth more difficult for a first child than for subsequent ones. We're not sure who said this first but somebody finally said, "Mary, the angel was right, it's a boy." And we're not sure who cleaned things up, but we assume there was a mess. There always is when a baby is born.

We assume that God could have provided for things to be different, a little neater maybe, maybe even an immaculate birth to go along with the immaculate conception, but had that happened we might have misunderstood completely what tonight is about. The messiness of a birth becomes a metaphor for what life is really like. Tonight the Almighty has come to us in flesh and blood, in muscle and bone, in all the glory and challenge of being human, and the appearing of this One speaks to all of us who move about in our flesh and blood, and muscles and bones, with all our joys and troubles of living as human beings with one another.

Of course giving birth is a messy thing, but so is living with each other after birth. It's a messy thing to be in this world with one another, to bump into each other's ideas, and to disagree with one another's opinions, and to get in the way of each other's plans. Giving birth is no messier than learning to live with each other, and work with each other, and get along with each other despite our different wants and needs. There's nothing neat about trying to get along in a work place or a church or a school or a family. Some days we are thrilled to be together, and some days we want to scream. Some days we bring each other joy and laughter, and some days we hurt each other. It's a little messy on the best of days.

The preference might be for us to meet Jesus in a textbook, or in a rainbow, or a waterfall, or a poem, anything that is less messy than dealing with other human beings. Our preference might be for us to meet each other the same way — in a book, or at a waterfall, or through some story. Maybe that would satisfy the folks who find the incarnation to be a little too earthy. Clearly some would like it if we could keep Jesus and each other on a theoretical level. But that isn't how God meets us, and that's not the way we meet each other. Just as the Word became flesh and lived among us, so we in our flesh find ways to construct and sustain human community, despite the messiness.

Do you remember that 1970s number by Paul Simon and Art Garfunkel called "I Am A Rock"? It's the kind of song that is the antithesis of tonight. In some ways it is depressing, but I suspect most of us have been to the point of wanting to distance ourselves from other people because we get so tired of each other at times. The song talks about trying to get around the messiness and pain. It begins, "I am rock, I am an island," and includes lines like, "I have no need of friendship, friendship causes pain, it's laughter and it's loving I disdain." The song talks about surrounding ourselves with walls that people cannot penetrate and of not waking the thought of love from the mind's slumber. Sometimes the messiness of living after the birth is much greater than the messiness at birth.

Mark Edwards recently retired as president of St. Olaf College in Minnesota and has been writing reflections on this www-dot world we live in.[1] Apparently those who find the flesh and blood of Christmas and of everyday life to be too messy and too much of an inconvenience have a way out. Just log on to any number of virtual churches on the worldwide web. One church in Evansville, Indiana, has a web site that allows people to experience worship without ever leaving the comfortable chair in front of the computer.

Links include taking the visitor into a chat room with the pastor for more information about the church, opportunities to have marriage counseling on-line, the chance to talk with elders of the church about being baptized, and a trip into the sanctuary for a "virtual worship service." You can even click on the link marked "Donation" and tithe just like the people who are actually there. (Somehow we knew that link would be there.) Edwards says the music isn't bad and you can join worship at any time. With tongue in cheek, he says the audio and video aren't great, but the convenience of being able to stay in your home and avoid the crowds makes up for the lack of quality in the presentation.

Lately we have heard about a lot of things being "virtual": virtual universities, virtual churches, virtual malls, virtual everything. But what does that mean? In short, it means that some people have found the messiness too much. They have found the community of incarnation to be too draining and too frustrating, but they still want to give the appearance of being interested, involved, and even committed.

The birth we celebrate tonight was no virtual birth; it was real. And the life we are called to share by this birth is not about a virtual religious community, but a real community where we rub elbows with one another, smell each other's hair spray and perfume, notice the warts and big feet, and deal lovingly and hopefully with the flaws that come with being flesh and blood.

Joining a computer church may be just the answer for some, but some of us would miss the smiles and the hugs and the love we are so certain of behind those smiles and hugs. Logging on to www.praisejesus.org might solve some of our problems and ease some of our frustrations, but we wouldn't want to be down on our luck and waiting on a computer to stop by to offer encouragement.

If we surf the web enough we could probably find virtual friends to join us at our virtual church, but how would we fill the holes in our lives of not hearing people shuffle forward to take communion on Christmas Eve? And what would replace the fleshy handshakes of real people? And what about our other senses? The smell of this room. The vividness of the poinsettias. The light of candles bouncing off rich wood. The memories attached to the people and events here.

Edwards asks in his article, "Does the loss of real presence in worship and in church life matter, either to God or to the worshiper?"[2] We have come here tonight because we believe it does matter, both to God and to us. We gather here on all kinds of occasions to sit beside other living, breathing, thinking human beings, even as God has chosen to rub elbows with us.

Technology has given us so many advantages. Folks in remote areas are receiving college educations from accredited schools because of on-line classes. E-mail allows us to communicate cheaply and with great convenience. Information can be retrieved from the web that just years ago would have required hours and hours in a library somewhere.

But everything has its limits. The intersection between God and us does not happen at a stop along the information super highway, but in the messiness of a baby being born. And while we might catch up with each other by way of e-mail and other internet conveniences, those are meetings that lack the depth and the richness and the texture of face-to-face encounters. The incarnation with all its drawbacks still holds more joy and fulfillment than lives lived away from each other because of fear and frustration.

And even if we will never be convinced of that, there is still a God who is convinced. It is the practice of that God never to let individuals tarry too long by themselves. Even when something spectacular happens in the life of a person, scripture tells us that the next thing God always does is to usher the person by the arm into a community, saying, "Here, I would like you to meet some more of my people."

Of course God could have provided for things to be different, but think about the things we would have missed out on. They are worth a little messiness here and there.

---

1. Mark U. Edwards, Jr., "Virtual Worship," *The Christian Century*, December 6, 2000.

2. *Ibid.*

- 7 -

Not A Word To Anyone

Psalm 30* and *Mark 1:40-45

"Not a word to anyone." That's what Jesus told the leper after healing him. It is perhaps the strangest part of such a brief yet complex story. Lepers were required in those days to keep their distance from other people, but this one walked right up to Jesus, kneeled beside him, and begged to be made clean. Jesus should have known better; after all, leprosy was something that could be passed to another person just from the contact between two people's clothing, but here Jesus reaches out his hand and touches the man. All the rules seem to go out the window in these stories, including this warning Jesus gave the man: "Not a word to anyone about this. Don't tell a soul."

Curious indeed. In other places, Jesus gave instructions that are exactly opposite this stern command to tell no one. After Jesus healed a demon-possessed man, he was told, "Return to your home, and declare how much God has done for you" (Luke 8:39). When Jesus was preparing his disciples to be sent out to do ministry in his name, he said, "What I say to you in the dark, tell in the light; and what you hear whispered, proclaim from the housetops" (Matthew 10:27). In another place, the Pharisees were trying to get the disciples to be quiet and Jesus said, "Even if they stopped talking, the stones would shout out" (Luke 19:40). It is as if nothing can stop good news from being announced, which makes Jesus' request to the man not to say anything to anyone even more difficult to understand. Why would Jesus say such a thing?

It is a popular notion that Jesus was employing some reverse psychology here. "I'll tell this fellow not to say a word about being healed and what will happen is that he will tell everybody!" Well, that is exactly what happened. Jesus said to keep a lid on it and the man broadcasted it everywhere. But aren't we concerned about Jesus using mind games with people in order to get them to do what he wants them to do? It doesn't paint a very nice picture of Jesus. We're not sure that we want to have much to do with that kind of Jesus, especially after all that insistence from him that we use straight-talk and not double-talk. Jesus is the one who said, "Let your yes be yes, and your no, no" (Matthew 5:37). Jesus' hope was that we would be up front with each other and that we would not play those games where we slice our words so thinly that it leaves the other person wondering what is really meant by them.

If anything, a theory of reverse psychology may reveal more about our own communication tendencies than anything else. The family member tells us not to fuss over him, but we have heard that enough to know that it really means: "I'll expect a telephone call every day at 7 p.m. and two calls a day on Saturday and Sunday." Or, we are pulling out of the driveway to go on vacation and our neighbor yells, "Have a good time and spend your money on yourself this year." Interpretation: "If you don't bring me back something nicer than what you brought last year, don't bother coming back." No, that doesn't sound much like Jesus. There must have been another reason why he told the man not to tell anyone that he was healed.

Maybe the man was told this because Jesus was overbooked as it was. We know how much illness and pain are a part of every day. It sounds like it was that way in Jesus' time. The needs of the people were many and apparently Jesus was meeting those needs in ways that others were not. That's great news, but Jesus would soon be overwhelmed if the word got out. Even in this passage we are told that the word spread so quickly that Jesus was no longer able to go into town openly. The name-recognition and the size of the crowds pushed him to stay out in the country, but even there people came from everywhere to find him. Also, Jesus might well have been concerned that his popularity would be interpreted in the wrong way. He wasn't interested in garnering attention for attention's sake, or boosting personalities, or building huge crowds, but about proclaiming the love and justice of God. We know Jesus often tried to get away to be by himself, so maybe he told the man to keep things quiet so Jesus could be free to move about and to have some life to himself.

But this was also the one who was continuously inviting people to himself. He couldn't quit inviting. Sometimes he called people by name from their particular stations in life. And for those times when he didn't have any one of us in mind but wanted to make sure we all knew we had a place in his company, he said, "Come to me, all you that are weary and are carrying heavy burdens, and I will give you rest" (Matthew 11:28).

Of course Jesus was overbooked, but he wasn't overwhelmed because of the attention he gave his soul. Jesus took time for himself. He made sure that his prayer life was one thing that did not get cheated. His public ministry was supported by the strength and focus that came from times of private meditation and reflection. Jesus didn't tell the man to be quiet about things because he didn't want people coming around. His purpose for being here was somehow to bridge the gap between heaven and earth, between God and humanity. So maybe there was another reason for this stern warning not to tell anyone.

Maybe there was the fear of controversy. We know Jesus encountered all kinds of opposition. People tried to trap him in his own words. People tried to sabotage his ministry. In the end, he had to choose between keeping his commitment to sharing God's love and truth on the one hand and losing his life on the other. Some of the Gospel stories read as if the cross were in sight from the very beginning, casting a long shadow over the good that Jesus was attempting to do. A lot of good things that ought to happen don't because we sometimes are afraid of stirring up trouble. We would think that everybody would be happy to see good things happen, but it isn't so. Worthwhile projects get shot down before they get off the ground. Dreams get criticized because somebody or some system is threatened by them. Sometimes we don't pursue things that we should because we think some issue or idea has a greater power to divide people than Jesus has power to unite us. What a shame.

But we can dismiss this idea, too. Jesus didn't go looking for trouble. He just didn't shy away from it. If he had eased up on his preaching, or hadn't insisted on keeping company with such lowlife, or hadn't made the Pharisees look like such religious lightweights, Jesus wouldn't have found himself in constant trouble with the religious and political leaders of the day. But he would have had to quit being Jesus, and he wasn't willing to sell out himself or the One who sent him.

Avoid controversy? No. He said to his disciples, "Friends, it's on to Jerusalem. I am going to suffer and die, but that won't generate half the controversy as my coming back to life." And what does he expect of us? Scripture says we are to do justice (Micah 6:8), and to do justice means we are going to name and address and eliminate the injustice and the unfairness in our community. There's not much way to do that and avoid controversy and Jesus knew that, so there must be some other reason for telling this former leper not to tell anybody about being healed.

So why, then? Why did Jesus tell this man not to tell anyone about what had happened? In that familiar passage of Ecclesiastes 3, the preacher says that there is "a time to keep silence and a time to speak" (Ecclesiastes 3:7). The tricky part, of course, is knowing which is which. Perhaps nothing reveals more about our maturity and our common sense and our good taste than knowing when it is time to keep silence and when it is time to speak.

Silence is powerful. How many families have been torn apart and how many individuals have been scarred forever because of some horrible secret that was never allowed to come to light? None of us wants to broadcast embarrassing and humiliating things about ourselves, but when abuse within a family is allowed to live under a blanket of silence it only leads to more abuse. Often, the abuse was swept under the rug and the victims lived for years with that silence. Silence is a powerful thing, and when it is inappropriate silence we should be prepared for lives to be destroyed. And like families, sometimes churches get trapped by silence, forfeiting the benefits of talking about things openly and honestly.

Silence is also a powerful thing in a good way. Perhaps the reason that Jesus told the healed leper to not tell anyone about what had happened, and why he told so many other people that very same thing, is because talking too quickly about something almost always means talking poorly about it. Jesus was saying, "You have just had a life-changing experience. You have encountered the living God in a way that has forever changed the way you see the world. You are a different person now. Take some time in silence, give a serious effort at beginning to understand what is going on, before you talk about it."

It isn't any accident that the verse from Ecclesiastes is arranged in the order it is. "There is a time to keep silence and a time to speak." First comes the silence. First comes the time of reflection on what has happened. First comes our attempt to deepen our own awareness of who we are and where we are and what is happening in our lives. First comes a clearer appreciation of what we are thinking and feeling. Then we can speak.

Holocaust survivor Elie Wiesel has written over thirty books. Almost all of them reveal something of his experience in Nazi concentration camps. However, Wiesel didn't speak or write a single word about those experiences for over ten years. After his release, he imposed a ten-year vow of silence on himself that did not allow him to say anything about what had happened. He knew he needed the time in silence first if he ever was to be able to make sense of and write about the Holocaust.[1]

Our everyday experiences are similar. Do you know of anything worse than talking through a beautiful sunset? The beauty of a sunset is not in our description of it, but in our remaining quiet and taking in its splendor. When somebody says to us, "I saw the most beautiful baby today," we can't say, "Really, what was so beautiful about it? Her hair? Her eyes? Her smile?" The person will respond, "Well, no, she didn't have any hair yet, and she was asleep so I didn't see her eyes or her smile." The beauty of a baby is not in the details that we can talk about, but in the miracle of life before us that leaves us speechless.

The mechanics of a deep, enduring friendship can be talked about, but not its beauty. We can say, "You know, we have always been there for each other and we talk and listen and laugh and cry." But whatever it is that brings us together, whatever chemistry that makes us close friends with this person and not that one, whatever it is that clicks when we are in the company of certain people that makes our world make a little more sense and seem a little less harsh, there aren't words for that, at least not at first. There is only the thanksgiving of silence.

On Sundays we incorporate some silence into the service, even though it is never enough. It is a good model for our daily lives to have some silence here so that we are reminded through the week of the importance of that silence. It is not a matter of our choosing not to say something, but of asking, "What is there to say?" If we believe prayer is some mysterious encounter with God, how could we do anything but be silent before and afterwards?

On other occasions of worship, on Christmas Eve and Maundy Thursday for instance, we are invited to leave the sanctuary silently. How else could we leave? The eternal God of the universe has become flesh to walk and live among us. What response could we make? Maybe, "You've got to be kidding," but perhaps simply leaving in humble silence is more reverent and gives us the greater chance of beginning to appreciate the miracle of all that. The Christmas hymn begins, "Let all mortal flesh keep silence, and with fear and trembling stand," which is the best way for "every heart to prepare him room." On Maundy Thursday we hear the story of Jesus being betrayed and denied and arrested and we know that he is hours from being killed. What does it all mean? All we know is that it is not the time for glib small talk and so we process out in stunned silence to go and cultivate a space in our lives where we can try to make sense of those events and of our own betrayals and denials.

Jesus told the man who was healed not to say a word to anybody. We too are invited to give attention to our souls, to cultivate an interior life that can support the exterior life. We too are given the opportunity to appreciate the sacred nature of words and to prayerfully consider what actions will best match those words. We too are invited into that silence where depth is cultivated, where there is no pressure to speak right away, and where being a patient friend of time leads to an understanding that mere talk cannot.

Hear again how the psalmist speaks of God. "Lord, you have drawn us up and did not let our foes rejoice over us. We cried to you for help, and you have healed us. You brought our souls up from Sheol and restored our lives" (Psalm 30:1-3). Ours is a great and loving God, able to do far more than we ever think to ask. Ours is a God who has transformed our lives. But don't tell anybody. Not yet.

---

1. Robert McAfee Brown, Preface for the Twenty-Fifth Anniversary Edition, *Night* (New York: Bantam Books, 1986), p. v.

- 8 -

To Care And Not To Care

Luke 3:15-22

The work of poet T. S. Eliot was as highly respected as anyone's work in the field of literature. He even won a Nobel Prize for literature in 1948. But following his conversion to Christianity, many critics considered Eliot's work suspect. Some folks felt a great sense of betrayal when Eliot became a Christian. Many found his works of gloom and despair far more appealing than the writings that made reference to the presence of God in his life.

In his poem "Ash Wednesday," there appears a curious and compelling line. It's really more of a prayer than a poem. It says, "Teach us to care, and not to care."[1] It's one of those phrases that has to rattle around in our minds for a while before we can get at its deep truths. A lot of poems and passages of scripture and songs are like that. Until we have some experience that brings the truth of some poem alive, some occasion of reflection that gets its wisdom out in the open where we can see it, the power of a statement lies dormant. "Teach us to care, and not to care" may fall into this category.

Clearly the easiest part of this prayer is the first part, "teach us to care," or at least we think that is the easiest part. After all, if Christians don't do anything else, we care. Churches who don't care about each other and care for each other aren't likely to remain churches very long, or at least not with any sense of vitality and enthusiasm.

We also like to think the "teach us to care" part is manageable because we live in a time when we probably know more about caring than people have known at any other time. Professional caregivers receive education and practical experience that are very thorough and in-depth. Magazines and self-help groups and internet resources inform us on the matter, telling us how to care for tiny infants and aging parents, passing along tips about how to help people with a recent heartache or disappointment, providing remedies for what ails any relationship, and showing us how to communicate with one another more effectively.

But just because we know more about caring doesn't mean we actually care more than we ever have. Some say we actually care less than we have in the past. Some are convinced we have all the appearances of caring, but that we don't really spend the time required to care for each other. After all, caring for one another is not an efficient thing. Our care for people may lead us to spend hours and hours with them over a period of many months or years. It's messy, it's frustrating, it's tiring, and it's a little frightening at times.

To care for people, to really nurture and guide people toward health and wholeness, carries with it the expectation that we will get involved with our hearts and minds and souls. To care for each other implies a level of engagement and attention that not everybody is comfortable with. And to care for people means one more thing. It means to be able to be with each other in our woundedness.

Maybe the baggage we are carrying stems from childhood trauma. Maybe the ache we feel is from a more recent break-up. Maybe our regrets have piled up and the guilt is depressing us. Maybe the years have done nothing to ease the loss of a loved one. Maybe our employment is at a low point. Maybe things at home aren't what they once were. Maybe the work of being a parent is a little overwhelming right now. Maybe the challenges of growing old are too real. Maybe the search for a soul mate is not yielding results.

We all carry some pain, some frustration, some disappointment. To care for each other is to be okay with open wounds and broken hearts and unfulfilled dreams, okay enough with those things to be present with each other. Caring for each other, in times of joy and sorrow alike, requires a level of attention and empathy that can deal with the tears and the cursing and the doubting and the questioning.

This little prayer is so important because that's not a level of care that comes naturally. The reason we pray that we be taught to care is because we know that the glossing over of human pain isn't really caring. We know that as nice as it is to have somebody stick his head in and say hello, that's only a part of caring. Caring is about sitting with someone, holding a person's hand, being present to a person's fears and hopes, however small or large they seem to us. For a time when we are increasingly isolated from one another, the prayer, "teach us to care," speaks to us who claim caring to be at the heart of who we are.

The other part of the prayer asks that we be taught how not to care. This is a prayer that will have a difficult time catching on in a culture that values the productivity of people. In some circles, people brag more about the hours worked than the hours spent with family. And even though we have more games now than ever before, we are a people who have lost touch with how important it is to play. We are so caught up in being efficient and productive that wasting time doing nothing is seen as being sinful instead of being Sabbath.

Al Franken has a wonderful quote on parenting. He believes that as a father he needs to have some quality time with his kids, but he also is committed to quantity time — big, fat, stinking, lazy quantity time of staying in their pajamas all day and having pillow fights and eating popcorn.[2] Another example is that scene from the movie *Pretty Woman* where the wheeler and dealer Edward, a driven man who admits he never was certain of his father's love, puts business on hold for a while and goes walking barefoot in the park.

Most parents do well to spend quality time with their children. And most business people work among near cut-throat competition to create jobs and produce products and deliver goods. But the second part of this prayer calls those folks, and all of us, away from those things long enough for us not to care for a little while.

The instructions from the psalm are to "Be still and know that I am God" (Psalm 46:10). It's a form of not caring long enough so that we can remember who we are and who God is. As humans, we have limits and boundaries that, when crossed, cause us trouble. We tend to lose our perspective unless we step back from time to time. We need to not overvalue ourselves or exaggerate our own importance. Without entering into a time of detachment, a time of not caring in our personal lives and in our family and work and school situations, we soon find ourselves without the energy and compassion to continue. Some call that burn-out. It's the process of losing our emotional, spiritual, physical, and mental resources at a much faster rate than they are being replenished.

We can only care for and about so much at any one time and still get on with living. And sometimes we overestimate the things we have any control over. Sometimes our not caring is really about letting go of some things. We have to be who we are and to be faithful to that. If we are swayed by criticism or by not being understood, or if people's gossip and half-truths bother us, or if we try to do more than we can do and the physical and emotional fatigue causes us not to be at our best for several weeks or longer, what good are we?

Sometimes churches fall into the trap of not stepping back. Churches have to learn not to care. Some committees and groups meet because the meeting is on the calendar, not because there is pressing need or great enthusiasm or clear purpose for the meeting. Churches, especially ones that fear they are dying, try to overcome their decline by working harder and staying busier. What an irony! It might have been the failure to be still and be in touch with God that put those churches in a tailspin to start with.

For one person, it was his mother's illness that caused him to reflect on this prayer. During a two-month hospital stay, the man's mother seemed near death on several occasions only to rally and appear to be on the road to recovery. She spent six weeks of the hospitalization in the intensive care unit. After the hospitalization, the woman spent over a month at a rehabilitation center before passing away.

People who have been through similar things know that really to be present with someone who is that sick requires a good bit of energy. What some find is that it also requires a good bit of time away from the person who is sick. As a way to ensure that the mother had ongoing attention and encouragement, and to ensure that the family members were able to provide that kind of care, the family members tried to arrange their schedules so that everyone had at least one day, and two whenever possible, away from the caring. It was a time not to care. Of course, the family members checked in by telephone and rarely did a minute pass without their mother's well-being surfacing in their thoughts, but time away gave them the opportunity, in a sense, not to care.

Today's Gospel lesson tells us of Jesus' baptism, which shaped and directed Jesus' life and ministry. We are reminded that our baptism shapes our caring and not caring. Our baptism calls us to care for and about certain things, and it calls us to leave certain things alone.

Jesus gave us an example of what it means to care and not to care. When he was with someone, that person had his full attention and interest. One day he received word that his friend Lazarus was near death. Instead of rushing right over to Bethany, Jesus stayed where he was for two more days. Even for Jesus, he could only care for and about so much. Before going to see Lazarus, Jesus' care was for someone else. He was delayed in getting to Lazarus, but the guarantee was that when Jesus got there, Lazarus and his sisters had his full attention and care (John 11:1-45).

Jesus also made it a point to get away from the crowds — to not care from time to time. For those times to be mentioned so often in scripture we have to assume that his getting away was an important part of who he was. The only way Jesus could care, really care, was to make sure there were times when he was not caring.

The story is told of an archbishop who went about his ministry day after day. Every afternoon he would go home and pray, and his words to God were something like, "There it is for today, Lord. I'm finished and I'm going to relax now. After all, it's your Church, Lord, and it's ultimately your responsibility. I worked today and that was okay, and I'll work again tomorrow, but I'm going to get some rest now and enjoy some more of the life you have given me."[3]

It's the gift of learning to care and not to care.

---

1. T. S. Eliot, *Complete Poems and Plays* (New York: Harcourt, Brace and Company, 1952), p. 61.

2. Al Franken, *Rush Limbaugh Is a Big Fat Idiot and Other Observations* (New York: Delacorte Press, 1996), p. 71.

3. Jean Vanier, *Community and Growth* (New York: Paulist Press, 1979), p. 210.

- 9 -

This Is My Life

The poet William Stafford writes:

> *Some time when the river is ice ask me*
> *mistakes I have made. Ask me whether*
> *what I have done is my life. Others*
> *have come in their slow way into*
> *my thought, and some have tried to help*
> *or to hurt: ask me what difference*
> *their strongest love or hate has made.*
> *I will listen to what you say.*
> *You and I can turn and look*
> *at the silent river and wait. We know*
> *the current is there, hidden; and there*
> *are comings and goings from miles away*
> *that hold the stillness exactly before us.*
> *What the river says, that is what I say.*[1]

"Ask me whether what I have done is my life." Stafford must have known that sometimes we can get so caught up in trivial things or so sidetracked in distractions that we don't get around to doing the things that we want our lives to be about. Our days are still full, but we seem to be counting the days instead of having days that count. Our calendars and schedules point to any number of things we are involved in, but those events and activities don't always reflect what we want our lives to be about. "Ask me," Stafford said, "ask me whether what I have done is my life."

In that line there is no requirement that all of our lives look alike. Your life will be different from mine, and the lives of others will be different from ours. This isn't about a dull uniformity, but about each of us finding that particular and authentic expression of living that best fits us as unique creations of God. Jesus' words were to "let *your* light shine" (Matthew 5:16). We each have a part of the light, and in these words Jesus gives us the freedom to show forth the light that we each have been given. And in doing so, the Light takes on a new wholeness.

Certain occasions cause us to think about whether what we are doing is really our life. When the last member of the older generation passes and we are left to carry on the family name and sustain the family tradition, we often stop and reflect on the shape of our lives. When a relationship ends and the individuals are trying to reclaim their own identities after being enmeshed in each other's for so long, it is another opportunity to consider afresh what our lives are really about. When churches celebrate significant occasions, such as anniversaries of their ministry, or the loss of someone who held the congregation together, the time is ripe for asking whether what we are doing is our life.

Jesus must have known that there were all kinds of ways he could spend his time, but in the end he wanted the assurance that what he had done was really his life, his passion, his driving concern. Before beginning his ministry, he made a public announcement about the things and the people that would be most important to him. If ever there was a keynote that set the tone for something, if ever there was an opening statement that charted the direction and identified the agenda, this is it.

And where else would Jesus turn for understanding his mission than scripture? After his baptism, and after some time in the wilderness trying to understand what that baptism meant, Jesus stood in the synagogue and read from his favorite prophet, Isaiah: "The Spirit of the Lord is upon me, because he has anointed me to bring good news to the poor. He has sent me to proclaim release to the captives and recovery of sight to the blind, to let the oppressed go free, to proclaim the year of the Lord's favor" (Luke 4:18-19).

Jesus said, "This is what I am going to be about. This is what my life is. And I will not get sidetracked or distracted and I will not allow myself to be overwhelmed with things that do not matter. Nothing will be as important to me as bringing good news to the poor and setting people free from the chains that bind them."

It makes sense for this to be what Jesus is about because this is what God is about. Jesus didn't say, "Okay, let's see, what can I do? What are my interests? What are the things I would like to see done?" No, Jesus said, "It's not so much that I have a mission, but that God has a mission and I have been called to participate in it." Jesus' way of showing that was to read from Isaiah, to ground himself in the tradition of the prophets, and to offer himself to things that God has always been about.

When Jesus talked about setting the captives free, there's no doubt that he was as concerned about the political reality as he was about matters of the heart. The hope for a messiah in those days — and there were a lot of would-be messiahs — was not only that things would be set straight in the religious realm, but in every arena of life — political, economic, cultural, religious — everything! So Jesus talked about a God who longs to set people free from public policies that oppress people, systems that keep people in bondage, and attitudes that cause one group of people to hold power over another group. And the promise of freedom is a gift for us as individuals, so that we might be able to live our true lives.

A lot of things can get in the way. We might still go through the motions. We might even get a lot done, but we know in the quiet places of our own souls whether what we are doing is really our life. We may even know what it is that is holding us back. We might even be able to point to the place along the journey where we got stuck, but doing something about it can be a difficult process.

Guilt over some decision or action can nearly paralyze us, and the longer we hold on to it the more power it has. God forgives us, and we are willing to forgive each other, long before we are willing to forgive ourselves. Listen to the way Don Miguel Ruiz describes it in his wonderful little book *The Four Agreements*:

> *True justice is paying only once for each mistake. True injustice is paying more than once for each mistake. The human is the only animal on earth that pays a thousand times for the same mistake. The rest of the animals pay once for every mistake they make. But not us. We have a powerful memory. We make a mistake, we judge ourselves, we find ourselves guilty, and we punish ourselves. If justice exists, then that was enough; we don't need to do it again. But every time we remember, we judge ourselves again, we are guilty again, and we punish ourselves again, and again, and again.*[2]

Guilt can keep us from our true lives. Jesus says that God wants the captives of guilt to be set free.

A lot of folks are so enslaved to what others think of them that what they do usually is not their life, but someone else's. Whether it be the need for someone's approval or the fear of someone's criticism, we sometimes find ourselves trapped by what other people want for us. Jesus says that God's love for you and me as we are is so great that the captives of other people's expectations can be set free.

The fear of death and suffering and pain can hover over us like a cloud to the point that we prefer the shadow, even when we can see the sun shining not far from us. We find ourselves buying into our great cultural denial about death. We think we can face anything except death, but what we soon find is that until we face up to death we aren't free to face anything else. Jesus says that God's love and care for us does not stop when our breathing stops, so all the captives of the fear of death can be set free.

The greater fear than death is life. We are often much more afraid of living, of really giving hearts and souls to something or someone, than we are of dying. We are fascinated by ordinary people who take on great challenges and life-changing projects, but not so fascinated that we move out of our fear of living long enough to try to do one ourselves. We are glad some people still have an adventurous spirit and a bold courage, but we would rather not disrupt a comfortable (read: boring) life. Jesus says that God wants you and me to have an abundant life, not just a long one, and so God sets free the captives who are afraid to really live.

Grief and loss hold such sway over our lives. Some of it has to do with how much we miss someone we love. Some of it has to do with getting used to the fact that life doesn't always bend to our wants and wishes. Some of it has to do with facing our own mortality and finiteness. The whole grief process is something of a mystery, but what we do know is that it isn't very neat. There may be stages, but they aren't so predictable that we all go through them in the same way. It's not a matter of the pain going away and us resuming the journey. It's more like the healing comes to us as we continue the journey. Jesus says that God cares for the birds of the air, so how much more must God care for us, and how much more must God want all the captives of grief and loss to be set free.

Some individuals and a lot of churches are slaves to small dreams and short-term vision. We tend to think in tiny little compartments and about tiny little periods of time, but what we do and decide now will affect the lives of many people who will come after us. Every generation has the opportunity to pave the way for really great things or for really lousy things. Every generation either makes life for those who follow them a lot easier or a lot harder. Jesus says that the kingdom of God has come near enough to all of us to set free the captives of puny ideas and make-do plans.

And whatever else we are captive to, all our problems, including the real ones, are opportunities for God's freeing presence to be made known. Think about our jealousy, the misery we enjoy, the limitations we impose upon ourselves, the preoccupation with other people's business, the wasted focus on things that don't matter much in the long run. Jesus says, "The Spirit of the Lord is upon me. He has sent me to proclaim release to the captives."

Our lives and the life of our churches include some mistakes, but our life isn't about those mistakes. There's pain and brokenness and disappointment in our lives, but that's not what our lives are about. There's fear and uncertainty and anxiety in our lives, but that's not what our lives are about either.

Of all the images that people have of God, then and now, Jesus sought to clarify those by telling people that God wants you and me to know healing and wholeness and purpose. This is a God whose heart breaks when God's children are captive to anything that keeps them from knowing what their life really is. This is a God whose spirit cringes when God's children are so broken and fearful that they can no longer believe in their passion.

We are invited to live in the reality of God's promise of freedom, to experience the burden being lifted, the path being cleared, and the obstacle being pushed out of the way. We are led to refuse whatever has unrightfully taken claim on our lives and to reclaim our lives as God has created them to be. Grady Nutt used to tell the story of a goldfish being taken out of its bowl and being placed in a larger body of water. What Nutt said is that for several minutes the goldfish will continue to swim in tiny, little circles because it has not yet learned of the vastness of the pool. Being captive to any of these things we have talked about here is like maintaining the tiny, little circles long after that is necessary.

Jesus says that God wants the captives to be set free, and not just because we all are called to experience personal fulfillment and individual satisfaction. To follow Jesus of Nazareth is to be at work on behalf of others in their captivity. Whether it be political or economic or racial or cultural bondage, or whether it be spiritual or emotional or psychological captivity, none of us is really free until all of us are free. What a wonderful name those civil rights workers had in the 1960s — the Freedom Fighters. That's who we are. We can't be followers of Jesus without taking up the causes of Jesus, and Jesus came to set the people free. Churches worth being a part of are churches that announce that God is still about God's business and that we are participating in that activity of God by giving ourselves to the freedom of all of God's children.

At some point even God must say, "Ask me whether what I have done is my life." And then God looks around and the poor are at the banquet table, the blind are seeing, the deaf are hearing, the lame are dancing, and all the captives have been set free. And God says, "Yes, this is my life. This is my life."

1. William Stafford, *The Way It Is: New and Selected Poems* (St. Paul, Minnesota: Graywolf Press, 1998), p. 56.

2. Don Miguel Ruiz, *The Four Agreements* (San Rafael, California: Amber-Allen Publishing, 1997), p. 12.

- 10 -

I'll Take Two Of Whatever He Has

2 Kings 2:1-12

Of all the things that lead to a deeper faith, things like reading the Bible, praying, serving, and the like, there is one that may make more difference than any of the others. If we really want to grow in our faith, we should get close to someone who has a deep and lively faith.

Talk of love fills the pages of scripture, but it often sounds unbelievable until we encounter the compassion and attention and interest of another person. Hope finds its way into nearly every situation in the Bible, but it becomes much more real to us when we are in the same room with somebody who is fighting the good fight and keeping the faith in the face of long-shot odds. Hymns and sermons and prayers promote joy, but not as convincingly as people who live daily with an irrepressible song in their hearts.

A few years back, in an effort to ensure that Michael Jordan would be able to live off his meager earnings from his basketball career, Nike helped out by using in one of their commercials the advertising slogan, "I want to be like Mike." Most people who have laced up a pair of tennis shoes and dribbled a basketball and taken a few shots have thought about what it would be like to have the basketball skills of Michael Jordan.

We say similar things about people whose faith we respect and appreciate. "Oh, how I wish I could have the patience and understanding of that mother." "Gosh, I wish I had the inner calm that he does." "I wish I could muster the courage to take a stand on those issues." "I wish I would take the time to pray silently every day like she does." "I wish my attitude could be as positive as his." "I wish I could learn not to judge people so quickly and unfairly."

We see those kinds of qualities in other people and desire them for ourselves, but they are hard things to come by. This great old story about Elijah and Elisha says as much. Elijah is about to be taken up by God in a mighty whirlwind. Apparently everybody knows it. Everywhere they go people are saying to Elisha, "Did you know this is the day? Elijah won't be with us much longer." And each time, Elisha responds, "Yes, I know, but do we have to talk about that right now?" Finally, when the time is close, the established, venerated prophet Elijah asks his would-be successor Elisha, "Is there anything that I can do for you before I am taken from you?"

Imagine that moment. Maybe some of us don't have to imagine that moment. Some of us have been there. Good-byes are heart-wrenching. Around a hospital bed in the hospice unit, "Is there anything I can do for you before I am taken from you?" Just before pulling out of a college campus and leaving a child two thousand miles from home, "Is there anything I can do for you before I am taken from you?" Before friends, neighbors, or co-workers end up halfway around the world from each other, "Is there anything I can do for you before I am taken from you?"

Elijah asked. He said, "Is there anything that I can do for you before I am taken from you?" And Elisha answered not with specific requests about how to speak to people, or how to interpret God's word, or where to start in making necessary reforms, or what issues to raise with the authorities. No, Elisha's request was this: "Please let me inherit a double share of your spirit." Elisha could have asked for most anything, we suppose, but instead of asking for something specific that would have been adequate for one situation, he asked for the thing that would suffice in all situations. "Please let me inherit a double share of your spirit."

Elisha saw in Elijah something that Elisha needed if he was to accomplish what he was being called to do. Elijah had spoken boldly against the people's idolatry. In great faith Elijah had put his God up against the gods of Baal and had won. He had outsmarted and outmaneuvered Queen Jezebel. Time after time Elijah's love for God's ways fueled daring moves on God's behalf. Elijah was an enormously popular, even legendary, figure, a prophet among prophets. He had taken Elisha under his wings as a servant and had begun to groom him as a prophet.

When Elijah first ran upon Elisha, Elisha was plowing behind twelve yoke of oxen. Elijah called and Elisha said, "Okay, but first let me kiss my folks good-bye." Elijah said, "Do you not realize that you are being called to something very important? Let's get on with it." And then, in a stunning example of bridge-burning which symbolically and literally separated him from his former life, Elisha slaughtered the oxen, boiled their flesh, and gave it to the people to eat. "If I'm going with Elijah I won't need these anymore. Besides, it will probably do me good not to have that safety net of being able to return if things don't go well. This way, I am committed, heart and soul. There's no turning back" (1 Kings 19:19-21, with a bit of speculation and interpretation by the preacher).

Wherever Elijah went, there was Elisha. It's the kind of loyalty that we could stand to hear and see more of. But Elisha's constant presence at the side of Elijah was more than an expression of loyalty. If Elisha is like the rest of us, and we assume he was, surely a part of what is going on in this story is that Elisha is soaking up everything he can from Elijah before Elijah is taken away. "I will not leave you" can be a statement of need. "I will not leave you because I continue to draw on your strength. I need your presence in my life. I am still a little uncertain and afraid about all of this."

We can't throw away scripture and we can't stop praying. We still need to worship and serve. But the one thing that will help a lot of this other make sense is identifying somebody whose faith is strong and staying close to that person's side.

Sponsors play a critical role in Alcoholics Anonymous. Sponsors work with people who are new to the program, people who have just become sober, and help them work the twelve steps toward experiencing and understanding God. Sponsors are people who have already worked the twelve steps. In other words, they have been there. They know what it is like to become sober, to move through the twelve steps, and to take their lives back. They are the people most qualified to help others. In a way, those are the kinds of folks we are looking for to go with us on our faith journey. The person whose faith often appeals to us is the person who has been through the horrible mess and has come out on the other side without becoming mean or negative or nasty.

We shouldn't miss a really important clue in the story. We remember that any time someone's name is mentioned in scripture, it is like a red flag waving at us. A lot of people are never named in scripture, so when someone is named we know the name may be a clue to what is going on in the story. The name "Elijah" means "Yahweh is God." That is the attraction! Elijah exhibited a faith that announced to the people around him, "My God is the One who is always present, the One who calls people and all of creation into a holy covenant, the One who ultimately rules over history."

That is what Elisha wanted a double share of. It wasn't just that Elijah had a good personality or handled himself well in tight spots. Elijah knew God. Elijah lived out of a God-center. Elijah saw the world as God sees it and as God wills for it to be. It is only natural that Elisha would ask, "Please let me inherit a double portion of your spirit."

Other clues exist about why Elisha wanted a double share of Elijah's spirit. What about Elijah's encounter with God at Mount Horeb? The word came to Elijah, "Go out and stand on the mountain before the Lord, for the Lord is about to pass by." A mighty wind blew by and it was so strong that it was splitting mountains and breaking rocks, but God was not in that wind. Then there was an earthquake, but God was not in the earthquake. Then came a fire, but God was not in the fire. And then there was silence, and Elijah knew that was God in the silence.

We are drawn to anybody whose spirit is fed by the silence. We live with enough strong winds and enough earthquakes and enough fires. We want to keep company with people who resist being shaped by the daily bombardment of noise and glitz and hype and instead spend time in the silence. There is something about Elijah's faith being strengthened by the silence that invited Elisha and invites us all to come away from the noise and spend time centering ourselves in the stillness of the day. For there in the silence, God meets us. There in the silence we are told again who we really are. There in the silence life regains order and perspective and meaning.

But why did Elijah say that Elisha had asked for a hard thing? If the need for a double portion of a deep and lively spirit of faith is so great, why make it a hard thing to get? People who are facing surgery and recovery and treatments need a double portion of the spirit of healing and strength. People who have been wronged need a double portion of the spirit of peace and wholeness. People who have wronged others need a double portion of the spirit of forgiveness and mercy. People who are facing some great challenge need a double portion of the spirit of courage and perseverance.

So with the needs so great, why is granting the request of a double spirit such a hard thing to do? Because, unlike much of what we consume and experience in our culture, faith does not grow from a tiny seed to full flower overnight. The people whose faith we respect and appreciate and desire for ourselves did not develop one morning during Sunday school or one afternoon during a Circle meeting or one night at a discussion group. A deep and lively faith comes over time, through good moments and bad, and by giving attention to it. Faith comes by being in worship even when there are no bright flashes of revelation. Faith comes by immersing ourselves in the silence, even when there is not time to do so. Faith comes by singing the words of hymns, even when they don't seem to be very relevant. Faith comes by turning the pages of the sacred story, even when there are no burning bushes in our own understanding.

We do not arrive at a major intersection of life and quickly cultivate our faith. Rather, we prepare for that major intersection, even when we don't know when or what it is going to be, by paying attention to our souls and to the God who lives in and among us. What great opportunity lies ahead? We don't know, but we know the faith that will be required for it cannot be produced on the spot. What great sorrow lies ahead? We don't know that either, but we know that it will require of us a faith that has grown through the years.

There have been times in our lives when we have asked for a double portion, but when we realized what was involved we politely said, "No, thank you." There have been times in our lives when challenges have called for a double portion, but we have tried to do it on our own. There have been times in our lives when we were surrounded by faith-filled people, but did not take advantage of the strength and direction that come from such a group.

But there also have been those times when we did recognize faith in others and set out to make it our own. Elisha did it. Elisha took Elijah's mantle upon himself and struck the Jordan River and, just as it had done with Elijah, the water parted to one side and the other, and Elisha crossed over. And when the prophets who were at Jericho saw Elisha coming at a distance, do you know what they said? They declared, "The spirit of Elijah rests on Elisha."

May the same be said of us.

www.ingramcontent.com/pod-product-compliance
Lightning Source LLC
Chambersburg PA
CBHW071751040426
42446CB00012B/2519